THE THIRD BOOK OF CATHOLIC JOKES

THE THIRD BOOK OF CATHOLIC JOKES

GENTLE HUMOR ABOUT AGING AND RELATIONSHIPS

Deacon Tom Sheridan
Foreword by Father James Martin, SJ

acta
PUBLICATIONS

THE THIRD BOOK OF CATHOLIC JOKES
Gentle Humor about Aging and Relationships
by Deacon Tom Sheridan
with a Foreword by Father James Martin, SJ

Edited by Gregory F. Augustine Pierce
Editorial assistance by Mary Eggert, Donna Ryding, Mary Pierce
Cover design by Tom A. Wright
Text design and typesetting by Patricia A. Lynch

Published by ACTA Publications, 4848 N. Clark Street, Chicago, IL 60640, (800) 397-2282, www.actapublications.com

Library of Congress Catalog number: 2011927343
ISBN: 978-0-87946-461-5
Printed in the United States of America by Total Printing Systems
Year 25 24 23 22 21 20 19 18 17 16 15
Printing 15 14 13 12 11 10 9 8 7 6 5 4 3 2

♻ Text printed on 30% post-consumer recycled paper

CONTENTS

CONTENTS

DEDICATION

This book of humor is dedicated to the everyday people in the pews. In these times when the Church is stressed by pressure from without and turmoil from within, a good dose of laughter can sometimes put things back in perspective and remind us that God really is in charge.

FOREWORD
by Father James Martin, SJ

Laughter is an underappreciated virtue in the Christian spiritual life. Too many well-meaning and otherwise thoughtful believers equate being religious with being deadly serious. But, as the saying goes, when you're deadly serious you're probably seriously dead.

It's not clear how the idea that laughing is somehow "anti-religious" gained currency in Christian circles, but it may go back to the fact that there are no recorded instances in the Gospels of Jesus laughing. But Jesus *must* have laughed. Anyone who told clever parables and amusing stories, and who put up with his rather exasperating band of disciples, must have had a well-developed sense of humor.

One of my favorite little "proofs" for this belief is the story of Nathanael. In the Gospel of John (1:43-51) there's a wonderful little narrative in which Jesus decides to go to Galilee, where he meets up with a man named Philip and says to him, "Follow me." Later, Philip meets up with his friend Nathanael, and shares some surprising news. He tells his friend that he has found the Messiah. At the end of what must have been a breathless and excited conversation, Philip announces that the Messiah is from Nazareth.

Nathanael, who was apparently a difficult man to impress, says blandly, "Can anything good come from Nazareth?"

Though we often overlook the widespread humor in the Bible,

Nathanael's quip is clearly a joke about the small town of Nazareth. Some Scripture scholars say that at the time, Jesus's hometown was a backwater village with as few as fifty families. It's like saying, "Oh really? Nazareth? You're kidding, right?"

Later Jesus meets up with the fellow who made light of his hometown. And what does he say in response? You might expect the dour, grumpy, depressed Jesus of popular imagination, the "Man of Sorrows," to say in solemn tones, "Make not fun of the town of Nazareth!" Or, "Woe to you who mock the poor town of Nazareth!"

But that's not what he says at all. Instead he says, with almost palpable joy, "Here is truly an Israelite in whom there is no deceit!" In other words, now *here's* a guy I can trust!

That little story shows three things. First, and most importantly, Jesus could appreciate a joke. It's one of many indications that he must have had a sense of humor. But let's look at it somewhat more theologically. If we believe that Jesus was fully divine and fully human (which we do believe), we must accept the fact that he laughed. For laughter is an essential part of a full, healthy and whole emotional life, an essential requirement for a "fully human" person.

The second thing that story demonstrates is that Nathanael obviously had a delicious sense of humor. In other words, one of the original apostles knew how to tell a joke and laugh a little.

Third, the evangelist (the fellow who wrote the Gospel, in this case St. John) must have had a sense of humor as well. After all, rather than expunging that witty dig at Nazareth, he preserved that little joke for all eternity.

So this little story shows that Jesus laughed; one of the apostles had a sense of humor; and St. John appreciated a funny story.

We forget these things at our peril. Laughter helps us to be human. Laughing at our own foibles reminds us not to take ourselves with such deadly seriousness. Laughter puts things in perspective: that's why so many of the saints laughed. St. Philip Neri, the 16th-century Italian saint, was known specifically for his sense of humor, and kept a sign above his door that read, "The House of Christian Mirth."

That's why *The Third Book of Catholic Jokes: Gentle Humor about Aging and Relationships* is so welcome. Any opportunity for us to laugh as Catholics, and to laugh at ourselves, is welcome. So read Deacon Tom Sheridan's wonderful new collection, and have a laugh – for God's sake. Literally.

INTRODUCTION

What is "Catholic humor?" That's a question I've been asked more than a few times because of the popularity of the two previous books in this series.

Indeed. What makes a joke "Catholic?" Is it subject matter? Or the characters? Or a bit of "inside" humor? Perhaps it's a little historical twist, or poking fun at a church authority figure or at ourselves?

Well, how about all of the above? And a lot more, actually.

Some people can really deliver a joke, especially some of my friends in sales and one or two clergy I've met, but I've never been a great joke-teller. Even after researching, discovering, and rewriting thousands of humorous bits for these books, I still sometimes stumble when telling one. I prefer stories from life, stories that are connected to the way we live, stories with that twist and a bit of the old-standby, irony.

But wait a minute. That's what jokes are: stories from life that have been re-framed and condensed into nuggets of humor.

Often, what make them identifiably "Catholic" are the traditions, the sensitivities, and the sensibilities of the reader. While many of the jokes in this book involve all the usual suspects, figures such as deacons, priests, and bishops and even the occasional parish council president or music minister and the like, it's the human situation behind the words that will connect us to the humor.

The Catholic character of a joke isn't always obvious. It shouldn't need to be. Catholics are funny when they're just being people. What makes a joke Catholic *can* be something as simple as that you wouldn't mind telling it to your 29-year-old pastor (now *that's* funny)…or your 86-year-old mother.

This volume meets that criterion. Growing older and maintaining relationships: What better opportunity is there to explore the humor that resides in life from a Catholic perspective? Here are identifiably Catholic jokes poking gentle fun at the people, practices, and premises that reflect who we are as a faith community with deep spiritual and historical roots. And, yes, there are Catholic clichés, because clichés flow from life and always have a ring of truth to them. And, yes, there are just plain old jokes about people and their foibles, jokes that see the humor in just being human – without being offensive or off-color. Jokes for Catholics and jokes about Catholics.

Inside this two-part book are jokes that reflect the humorous side of our relationships with one another and the comical perspective that comes with getting older. Enjoy them, share them with one another, and learn from them not to take yourself too seriously. As we Catholics say every Ash Wednesday, all we are is dust, and unto dust we shall return. In the meantime, we can share a good laugh.

Deacon Tom Sheridan
Ocala, Florida
Easter 2011

ABOUT THESE JOKES

This is the third volume of Catholic jokes. As in the first two books, the jokes gathered here have been collected from friends and other contributors, gleaned – and often polished – from various websites and other sources. Versions may be new or been circulated for ages. Some have been adapted from ones perhaps not specifically dealing with religion, but surely focused on the human condition, which Catholics – despite some evidence to the contrary – share with everyone else.

As stated in the first *Book of Catholic Jokes*, I believe all these jokes to be in what the lawyers call the "public domain," but if authorship or copyright of a particular joke can be determined, please let the editors know so it can be corrected and they can go to jail.

Will there be a fourth book of Catholic jokes? I don't know. There is something very Catholic about the number three. (Haven't you heard the one about the Trinity?) But four is a nice number, too, and so is seven and seventy times seven. So if you've got a favorite joke that you'd like to submit for another edition, please mail it to:

Deacon Tom Sheridan
The Book of Catholic Jokes
c/o ACTA Publications
4848 N. Clark Street
Chicago, IL 60640
800-397-2282, acta@actapublications.com
www.actapublications.com

PART ONE

Jokes about Aging

Laughter won't keep us from getting older, but it'll sure ease the pain.

There's an old and much-used bit of advice that says old age isn't for sissies. Surely there are travails as well as triumphs in aging, but getting older certainly beats the alternative!

The first time I knew I was an old guy – make that "mature American" – was when a young woman offered me her seat on a bus. I was on my way home from work at the Archdiocese of Chicago. Hey, I wasn't old; I hadn't even begun to think about retirement yet.

I turned her down, of course. But very nicely. Then I went home and looked in the mirror. The cliché is true: Inside every older person is a younger one wondering what just happened.

Several months later, another young woman offered me her seat on the same bus. I must have been tired, so I took it. That's why after I retired I stopped taking buses altogether. Bad for the ego.

Yes, the following jokes make fun of aspects of growing older, but it's when we lose our sense of humor and the ability to laugh at ourselves and even our growing frailties that we really begin to go downhill.

It takes courage, humility, and maturity to laugh at ourselves. So let's get to it.

**We don't stop laughing because we grow old;
we grow old because we stop laughing.**

An elderly couple is lying in bed one morning, having just awakened from a good night's sleep. He takes her hand and she responds, "Don't touch me. Call Father Bob. I want him to do the funeral."

"Why?" he asks.

She answers back, "Because I'm dead."

The husband says to her, "What are you talking about? We're both lying here in bed together and talking to one another."

The wife says, "No, I'm definitely dead."

Her husband insists, "You're not dead and I'm not calling Father Bob. What in the world makes you think you're dead?"

His wife answers, "Because I woke up this morning and nothing hurts!"

"Where is my Sunday paper?" demanded the little old lady calling the newspaper office.

"Madam," said the customer service representative, "today is Saturday. The Sunday paper will not be delivered until tomorrow, on Sunday."

There was quite a long pause on the other end of the phone, and the little old lady muttered meekly, "So that's why so few people were at Mass this morning."

It was dinnertime at St. Mary's Assisted Living Center. The man and woman, both widowed, had known each other for a number of years. The two were at the same table, seated across from one another.

As the meal progressed, he took a few admiring glances at her and finally gathered the courage to ask, "Will you marry me?" After about six seconds of careful consideration, she answered, "Yes. Yes, I will!"

The meal ended and, with a few more pleasant exchanges, they went to their respective apartments. Next morning, he was troubled. Did she say "yes" or did she say "no?" He couldn't remember. Try as he might, he just could not recall. Not even a faint memory. With trepidation, he picked up his phone and called her. First, he explained that he didn't remember things as well as he used to. Then he reviewed the lovely evening past. As he gained a little more courage, he inquired, "When I asked if you would marry me, did you say yes or did you say no?" He was delighted to hear her say, "Why, I said, 'Yes, yes I will' and I meant it with all my heart."

Then she continued, "And I'm so glad you called, because I couldn't remember who asked me."

Two women were discussing the upcoming dance at the parish senior citizens club. "We're supposed to wear something that matches our husband's hair, so I'm wearing black," said one.

"Oh, my," said the other, "I'd better not go."

After Mass on Sunday, my wife and I like to go out to breakfast. Last week we went to a new restaurant where the "seniors' special" was two eggs, bacon, hash browns, and toast for $5.99.

"Sounds good," my wife said. "But I don't want the eggs."

"Then, I'll have to charge you $7.49 because you're ordering a la carte," the waitress warned her.

"You mean I'd have to pay for not taking the eggs?" my wife asked incredulously.

"Yep," said the waitress.

"I'll take the special then," my wife said.

"OK, how do you want your eggs?" the waitress asked.

"Raw and still in the shell," my wife replied.

She took the two eggs home and baked a cake.

———

An elderly man, obviously inebriated, meets the parish's deacon and his wife coming out of a restaurant late one evening. The deacon asks where the man is heading. The man replies, "I am going to a lecture about alcohol abuse and the effects it has on the human body."

The surprised deacon responds, "Really? Who's giving that lecture at this time of night?"

The man replies sadly, "My wife."

As she was sitting in the waiting room for her first appointment with a new dentist, the woman noticed his diploma which bore his full name. Suddenly she remembered a tall, handsome, dark-haired boy with the same name had been in her class at Notre Dame High School more than 40 years before. Could he be the same guy that she had a secret crush on, way back then?

When the dentist came in the room, however, she quickly dropped that thought. This balding, gray-haired man with the deeply lined face was way too old to have been her classmate. Still, as he examined her teeth, she asked him if he had attended Notre Dame High School.

"Yes," he said with a certain pride.

"When did you graduate?" she asked. When he replied, she blurted out, "You were in my class!" He looked at her closely.

"I'm not sure. What did you teach?" he asked.

A couple of volunteers from the St. Vincent de Paul Society were delivering holiday goodies to some neighbors during a terrible blizzard. When they arrived at the home of two sisters who were well into their nineties, they were surprised to see the women pulling their car out of the garage. When asked where they were going in such a storm, they smiled and replied, "We're going to visit the elderly."

A sweet grandmother telephoned St. Luke's Hospital and timidly asked, "Is it possible to speak to someone who can tell me how a patient is doing?"

The operator said, "I'll be glad to help. What's the patient's name and room number?" The old woman replied, "Kate Murphy, Room 302."

The operator looked up the record and said, "Oh, good news. Her records say that Kate is doing very well. Her blood pressure is fine; her blood work just came back as normal and her physician has scheduled her to be discharged Tuesday."

The old woman said, "Thank you. That's wonderful! I was so worried! God bless you for the good news."

The operator replied, "You're more than welcome, Ma'am. Is Kate your daughter?"

The old woman replied, "No, I'm Kate Murphy in Room 302. No one tells me anything!"

———

"Oh God," sighed the wife one morning, "I'm convinced my mind is almost completely gone!"

Her husband looked up from the newspaper and commented, "I'm not surprised. You've been giving me a piece of it every day for fifty years now."

Bob and his wife, Carol, faithfully attend their parish's annual carnival every year where a local pilot would offer helicopter rides for a $50 donation to the parish building fund. And every year Bob would say, "Carol, I'd really like to ride in that helicopter." Carol always replied, "I know, Bob, but that helicopter ride is fifty dollars, and fifty dollars is still fifty dollars."

After several years of this, Bob said, "Carol, I'm 85 years old. If I don't ride that helicopter now, I might never get another chance." But Carol simply replied, "Bob, fifty dollars is still fifty dollars."

The pilot, a practical joker, overheard the discussion and said, "Folks, I'll make you a deal. I'll take the both of you for a ride. If you don't say a word for the whole ride, it won't cost you a penny! But if you say one word it's fifty dollars."

So up they went. The pilot made all kinds of fancy maneuvers, but not a word was heard from the back seat. He did daredevil tricks, but there wasn't a peep. As he landed, the pilot looked in the mirror and said, "Boy, I did everything I could to get you to say something, but you didn't. I'm impressed!"

Bob replied, "Well, to tell you the truth I almost yelled when Carol fell out, but you know, fifty dollars is still fifty dollars!"

**Eventually you reach a point
when you stop lying about your age
and start bragging about it.**

The man is up in years and he's concerned about his wife's hearing. He confides to his pastor one day, "Father, I think my wife's going deaf."

The priest answers, "Well, here's something you can try on her to test her hearing. Stand some distance away from her and ask her a question. If she doesn't answer, move a little closer and ask again. Keep repeating this until she answers. Then you'll be able to tell just how hard of hearing she really is."

The man goes home and tries it out. He walks in the door and says, "Honey, what's for dinner?" He doesn't hear an answer, so he moves closer to her. "Honey, what's for dinner?" Still no answer. He repeats this several times, until he's standing just a few feet away from her.

Finally, she answers, "For the seventh time, I SAID WE'RE HAVING MEATLOAF!"

———

The retired priest was in his 80s and moved into a nursing home before he was ready to admit he was getting old. What finally persuaded him?

"I was sitting in my rocking chair one day and couldn't get it going," he admitted.

Two elderly women were driving to Sunday Mass. Their car was large and both of them could barely see over the dashboard. As they came to an intersection, the stoplight was red but they just roared on through.

The woman in the passenger seat thought to herself: *I must be losing it. I could have sworn we just drove through a red light.*

A few minutes later the same thing happened: Right through the red light.

This time the woman was almost sure that the light had been red, so she decided to pay very close attention the rest of the way. Sure enough, at the very next intersection the light was definitely red and they sailed right through again. She turned to the other woman and said, "Mildred! Did you know you just ran through three red lights! You could have killed us!"

Mildred turned to her and said, "Oh, am I driving?"

———

Two golden-agers were discussing their husbands over tea.

"I do wish my Elmer would stop biting his nails. He makes me terribly nervous."

"My Billy used to do the same thing," the older woman replied. "But I broke him of the habit."

"How?"

"I hid his teeth."

Three older ladies invited their pastor to a Sunday dinner. After the meal they were sitting at the table chatting about various things. One woman said to the priest, "You know, Father, I'm getting really forgetful. This morning, I was standing at the top of the stairs and I couldn't remember whether I had just come up or was about to go down."

The second woman said, "You think that's bad, Father? The other day, I was sitting on the edge of my bed and couldn't remember whether I was going to bed or had just woken up!"

The third woman said, "I can't even remember what day it is, Father. Why, I missed church last Sunday because I thought it was Tuesday."

The priest smiled smugly. "Well, ladies, my memory's just as good as it's ever been, knock on wood," he said, rapping on the table.

Then he went to the front door and called out, "Who's there?"

The older a man gets, the more ways he learns to part his hair. Some men pull what little bit of hair they have around on their head to cover their baldness. However, as a man gets even older, he realizes there are basically only three ways to wear his hair: parted, unparted, and departed.

Re-released music for the parish senior citizens' party:

"You're So Varicose Vein," by Carly Simon

"How Can You Mend a Broken Hip?" by the Bee Gees

"The First Time Ever I Forgot Your Face," by Roberta Flack

"I Can't See Clearly Now," by Johnny Nash

"These Boots Give Me Arthritis," by Nancy Sinatra

"Once, Twice, Three Trips to the Bathroom," by the Commodores

"A Little Help from Depends," by the Beatles

"Rikki, Don't Lose Your Car Keys," by Steely Dan

"Mrs. Brown, You've Got a Lovely Walker," by Herman's Hermits

"Talkin' 'Bout My Medication," by the Who

"I Heard It through the Grape Nuts," by Marvin Gaye

———

**Some people try to turn back their odometers. Not me.
I want people to know why I look this way. I've traveled
a long way and some of the roads weren't paved.**

———

**The older we get,
the fewer things seem worth waiting in line for.**

The woman and her husband were at a group Reconciliation service at their parish. Because they were so frail, they went into the confessional together, and the woman tearfully admitted to the priest that she had shoplifted a can of peaches because she was hungry and forgot to bring cash with her to the store. The priest gently asked how many peaches were in the can. She sobbed and replied, "Nine."

The priest said that for her penance she would have to say nine Rosaries, "one for each peach."

Just then the woman's husband spoke up. "Father," he said, "she also stole a can of peas."

In the confessional, the elderly man says to the priest, "I am 92 years old, had a wonderful wife for 70 years until she died, and have many children, grandchildren, and great-grandchildren. Yesterday, I met two college girls hitchhiking. One thing led to another and I spent the night with them."

"Hmmm," says the priest. "Are you sorry for your sins?"

The man replies, "What sins?"

The shocked priest answers, "You know what you did was very sinful. What kind of a Catholic are you?"

"But I'm Jewish," replies the man.

"Then why are you telling me this?" says the priest.

"I'm 92 years old. I'm telling everyone I can," says the man.

"Hello, Mrs. Lyons," said the deacon as he visited the local senior citizen home. "How are you feeling today?"

"Well," she conceded, "I have shooting pains in my neck, dizziness, and constant nausea."

"That's too bad," said the deacon, making a note to himself. Then he added, "Your birthday is just next week, Mrs. Lyons. How old will you be?"

"Why, I'm going to be 39," the woman replied indignantly.

"Hmmm," muttered the deacon, making a note to himself, "Difficulty remembering simple math, too."

———

Did you hear about the 88-year-old man and the 79-year-old woman who got married at St. Monica's Catholic Church last week?

Did they throw rice at them?

No, they threw vitamin pills!

———

**You're getting old
when there's no question in your mind
that there's no question in your mind.**

An elderly woman was telling her daughter about a date with a 90-year-old man she met at the parish's senior citizens' group. "Believe it or not, I had to slap his face three times!" said the woman. "Do you mean that old man got fresh with you?" the daughter asked in disgust. "Oh, no!" her mother explained, "I had to slap him to keep him awake!"

Two elderly ladies had been friends for many decades. Over the years they had shared all kinds of activities and adventures. Lately, however, their activities had been limited to playing cards a few times a week at St. Mary's Senior Center.

One day, one woman looked at the other and said, "Now don't get mad at me. I know we've been friends a long time, but I just can't think of your name. I've thought and thought, but I can't remember it. Please tell me what your name is."

Her friend glared at her. For at least three minutes she just stared. Finally she said, "How soon do you need to know?"

Older people seem to read the Bible a lot more as they get older. They're cramming for their final exam.

Walking through the rear of the church one afternoon, the pastor came upon an older man sitting in a pew sobbing his eyes out. He asked the man what was wrong. He said, "I have a 22-year-old wife at home. She rubs my back every morning and then gets up and makes me pancakes, sausage, fresh fruit, and freshly ground coffee."

"Then why are you crying?" asked the priest.

He said, "She makes me homemade soup and my favorite brownies for lunch, cleans the house, and then watches sports TV with me for the rest of the afternoon. For dinner she makes me a gourmet meal with wine and my favorite dessert. And then she makes love to me until the wee hours."

"Well," said the priest. "That's wonderful. Why in the world would you be crying?"

"I can't remember where I live!" said the man.

Two older men were sitting in the reading room of St. Mary's Center. One said to the other, "How do you really feel? I mean, you're 75 years old. How do you honestly feel?"

"Honestly, I feel like a newborn baby. I've got no hair, no teeth, and I just peed on myself."

Despite his pastor's many sermons over the years about using talents and treasures wisely, a stingy older man was determined to disprove the saying, "You can't take it with you."

So when he was diagnosed with a terminal illness, he instructed his wife to go to the bank and withdraw enough money to fill two pillowcases. He then directed her to take the bags of money to the attic and leave them directly above his bed.

His plan: When he passed away, he would reach out and grab the bags on his way up to heaven. Months after the funeral, the wife, up in the attic cleaning, came upon the two forgotten pillowcases stuffed with cash.

"Oh, that old fool," she thought. "I knew he should have had me put the money in the basement."

————

The parish decided that a senior citizen fitness program would be a good idea to help people. After all, exercise is important as we grow older. Here's one keeping-fit suggestion they came up with:

Start by standing with a five-pound potato sack in each hand, extend your arms straight out to your sides and hold them there as long as you can.

After a few weeks, move up to 10-pound potato sacks, then 50-pound potato sacks. Finally you'll get to where you can lift a 100-pound potato sack in each hand and hold you arms straight out for more than a full minute!

Next, begin putting a few potatoes in the sacks.

Unexpectedly, the mother-in-law stopped by a newly married couple's house. When she rang the bell, her daughter-in-law opened it wearing not a stitch of clothes.

"What are you doing?" the mother-in-law asked.

"I'm waiting for my husband to come home from work," the daughter-in-law answered.

"But you're NAKED!" the mother-in-law exclaimed.

"This is my Love Dress," said the young woman.

"Love Dress? But you're naked!"

"My husband loves me to wear this dress! It makes him happy and it makes me happy. Please leave now, Mom, because your son will be home soon."

The mother-in-law left, but all the way home she thought about the Love Dress. When she got home she got undressed, showered, put on her best perfume, and waited by the front door for her husband to come home from the Knights of Columbus Hall.

He walked in, saw his wife standing there naked, and said, "What on earth are you doing?"

"This is my Love Dress," his wife replied.

"Needs ironing," he said.

**You know you're getting old
when everything either dries up or leaks.**

Early one Sunday morning, on her way to Mass, an elderly woman is pulled over for speeding by a young traffic cop.

Woman: "Is there a problem, officer?"

Cop: "Yes, ma'am, I'm afraid you were speeding. Can I see your license, please?"

Woman: "I don't have one, officer. I lost it four years ago for drunk driving."

Cop: "I see. Can I see your vehicle registration papers please?"

Woman: "I can't do that either, officer."

Cop: "Why not?"

Woman: "I stole this car, officer. Yes, and I killed and hacked up the owner."

Cop: "You what?"

Woman: "His body parts are in plastic bags in the trunk if you want to see."

The traffic cop calls for backup, and in minutes five police cars pull up, including the police chaplain who arrives to give the murder victim last rites. A police sergeant approaches the woman's car, clasping his drawn gun.

Sergeant: "Ma'am, please step out of your vehicle!"

The woman steps out: "Is there a problem, sir?"

Sergeant: "My officer says you have stolen this car and murdered the owner."

Woman: "Murdered? Are you serious?"

Sergeant: "Yes, please open your trunk."

The woman opens the trunk. "You see, sir. It's empty."

Sergeant: "Is this your car, ma'am?"

Woman: "Yes, here are the registration papers."

Sergeant: "My officer also claims that you do not have a driver's license."

The woman digs into her handbag: "That's silly, sir. Here it is."

Sergeant: "Thank you, ma'am, but I am puzzled. I was told by my officer here that you didn't have a license, stole this car, and murdered and hacked up the owner!"

Woman: "Sure, and I'll bet he also told you I was speeding."

**A frustrated wife told me the other day
her definition of retirement:
"Twice as much husband on half as much money."**

Did you hear about the 83-year-old woman on her way to church who talked herself out of a speeding ticket? She told the officer that she had to get there before she forgot where she was going.

A young priest stopped at a local fast-food joint for a quick cup of coffee when he noticed an elderly couple sitting down to lunch.

He saw that they had ordered a single meal and an extra drink cup. As he watched, the man carefully divided the hamburger in half, then counted out the fries, one for him, one for her, until each had half. Then he poured half of the soft drink into the extra cup and set that in front of his wife. The old man then began to eat, but his wife sat watching him with her hands folded in her lap.

The priest was touched and went up to them and asked if they would allow him to buy another meal so that they didn't have to split theirs.

The old man said, "Oh no, Father. We've been married 50 years, and everything has always been and will always be shared 50-50."

The priest then asked the wife why she wasn't eating. "It's his turn with the teeth first, Father."

———

The retired bishop, known for his passionate preaching, was very fond of pure, hot horseradish and made sure his housekeeper always kept a bottle of it on his dining room table. One day during an ecumenical luncheon, he offered some to the minister of a local evangelical megachurch, who took a big spoonful.

Some minutes later, when the minister was finally able to speak again, he gasped, "I've heard many of my fellow clergy preach hellfire, Your Excellency, but you're the first one I've met who passed out samples."

As soon as she had finished high school, a bright young girl named Mary shook the dust of Ireland off her shoes and made her way to New York City, where she became a successful show business performer.

Several years later she returned to her hometown for a visit and went to confession in the church she had attended as a child.

In the confessional, old Father Sullivan recognized Mary and asked her about her work. Mary explained that she was an acrobatic dancer. He wanted to know what that meant.

She said she would be happy to demonstrate what she did on stage and proceeded to step out of the confessional. With the old priest watching, Mary went into a series of cartwheels, leaping splits, handsprings, and backflips.

Kneeling near the confessional, waiting their turn, were two older ladies. Watching Mary's acrobatics with wide eyes, one said to the other, "Sure and will you just look at the penance Old Father Sullivan is givin' out this night, and me without me bloomers on!"

**When you are dissatisfied
and would like to go back to youth,
just think of algebra.
And the Latin Mass.**

Several older priests from a large Midwestern archdiocese and their cardinal archbishop were attending a retreat at a private countryside resort owned by a big donor. They were wandering around the grounds together in a group when they came upon an old bridge that crossed a quiet pond.

Unfortunately, they didn't notice the small sign declaring the bridge to be unsafe. As they began to cross it, a security guard came driving up. "Hey," he shouted. "You there! Get off that bridge!"

"It's all right," said the cardinal, taking charge. "We're at this resort with permission. We're Catholics."

"Maybe so," said the guard. "But if you don't get off that bridge, you'll all be Baptists!"

———

A man and a woman, both widowed, were residents of St. Patrick's Assisted Living Home. After a few years of deepening friendship, the man fell in love with the woman. He got down on his knee and said there were two things he would like to ask her.

She replied, "OK."

He said, "First, will you marry me?"

She answered "Yes" and then asked what his second question was.

"Will you help me up?" he asked.

Mike, 92, and Donna, 89, meet at the parish widows and widowers club and hit it off so well they decide to get married. During a stroll through town they pass a drugstore. Mike suggests they go in.

Mike asks the man behind the counter: "Are you the owner?"

Pharmacist: "Yes."

Mike: "We're about to get married. Do you sell heart medication?"

Pharmacist: "Of course we do."

Mike: "Medicine for arthritis?"

Pharmacist: "Definitely."

Mike: "Medicine for memory problems?"

Pharmacist: "Yes, a large variety. The works."

Mike: "What about vitamins, supplements, sleeping pills, Geritol?"

Pharmacist: "Absolutely."

Mike: "Everything for heartburn and indigestion?"

Pharmacist: "We sure do."

Mike: "You sell wheelchairs, scooters, walkers, and canes?"

Pharmacist: "All speeds and sizes."

Mike: "Great. We're using your store for our wedding gift registry."

The elderly abbot of a monastery somewhere in Colorado was known far and wide for his weather lore. He always seemed to know when a harsh winter was approaching. But the old abbot died and the new abbot lacked the old man's weather insights.

Still, the monks asked their new superior if the coming winter was going to be cold or mild. He didn't know, but to be on the safe side he told his community that the winter was indeed going to be cold and that they should make certain they had enough firewood.

But being a practical leader, he phoned the National Weather Service a few days later and asked, "Is the coming winter going to be cold or mild?"

"It looks like this winter is going to be quite cold," the meteorologist responded.

So the abbot went back to his monks and told them to collect even more firewood.

A week later, he called the National Weather Service again. "Does it still look like it is going to be a very cold winter?"

"Yes," the man at National Weather Service again replied, "it's going to be a very cold winter."

So the abbot again ordered the monks to collect every scrap of firewood they could find.

Two weeks later, he again called the National Weather Service. "Are you absolutely sure that the winter is going to be very cold?"

"Absolutely," the man replied. "It's looking more and more like one of the coldest winters we've ever seen."

"How can you be so sure?" the abbot asked.

The weatherman replied, "The monks up on the mountain are collecting a heck of a lot of firewood."

———

A deacon was called to a Catholic nursing home in Los Angeles to talk to a man who was thinking of marrying one of the other residents.

"Do you love her?" the deacon asked.

The old man replied, "I guess."

"Is she a good Catholic woman?"

"I don't know for sure."

"Does she have lots of money?"

"I doubt it."

"Then why on earth are you marrying her?"

"She can still drive at night."

———

**How old would you be
if others didn't know
how old you are?**

The president of the parish's St. Vincent de Paul Society asked his newest member, "Would you like to donate something to the home for the aged?"

"Yes," replied the man. "My mother-in-law."

The married couple, both 70 years old, was celebrating their 50th anniversary. That night, God appeared to them in prayer to congratulate them for their faithfulness and grant them each one wish.

The wife wanted to travel around the world. Poof! The wife had tickets in her hand for a world cruise.

Next, God asked the husband what he wanted.

He said, "I wish I had a wife 30 years younger than me."

Poof! The husband was 100.

An elderly gentleman walks into his parish's holiday party for senior citizens and gets a drink from the bar. Looking around, he spies an elegant woman his own age sitting alone at a table.

He sits down with her, takes a sip from his drink, and says, "So, do I come here often?"

Mary hadn't been to church lately, so her pastor decided to pay her a visit and see how the 85-year-old parish matriarch was doing. He knocked on her door and after a time he heard her spirited voice holler, "Hello, who is it?"

"It's Father Dave," he answered.

"Oh. Well, c'mon in," she said. "How are things down at the rectory?"

"Great! The Smiths had their little baby girl, and Mary and Tom got married. Everything is wonderful," the priest replied. "But I just wanted to see how you are doing. We've missed you."

"Well, I haven't been feeling too well lately. I had quite the root canal last month. The dentist is trying to save the few survivors."

Just then the phone rang and she excused herself to get it. The priest sat near a table with a magazine and a bowl of peanuts. After a few minutes, he began flipping through the pages. After another ten minutes or so, he began to get restless, so he started in on the bowl of peanuts while he read. He soon realized he had eaten the whole bowl.

Just then Mary returned and said, "I sure am sorry; that was my sister from Pittsburgh. She only calls once a month, so when she does we have to catch up on everything."

The pastor, feeling a little embarrassed, said, "I must also apologize. While you were gone I got hungry and ate all the peanuts in your little bowl there."

Mary replied, "That's OK, Father. Since the root canal, the best I can do is suck all the chocolate off 'em!"

At 75, the elderly pastor was finally retired and enjoying his one passion: fishing.

He was sitting in his boat when he heard a voice cry, "Pick me up; pick me up!" Looking around, he couldn't see anyone. He thought he was dreaming until he heard the voice again, "Pick me up." He looked in the water and there, floating on a lily pad, was a frog.

The priest said, "Are you talking to me?"

"Yes," the frog replied. "Pick me up, kiss me, and I'll turn into the most beautiful woman you've ever seen. I'll make sure that all your friends are envious and jealous because I'll be your bride!"

The priest looked at the frog, reached over, and picked it up carefully. Then he dropped the frog into his front pocket.

From the depths of the pocket, the frog cried out, "Are you nuts? Didn't you hear what I said? Kiss me and I'll be your beautiful bride."

The priest opened his pocket, looked down at the frog, and said, "Nah. At my age it's too late. I'd rather have a talking frog."

———

**I don't know how
I got over the hill
without getting to the top.**

Old Jonnie's parish celebrated his 100th birthday by throwing him a party. Everybody complimented him on how athletic and well-preserved he appeared.

"Gentlemen, I will tell you the secret of my success," he cackled. "I have been in the open air day after day for some 75 years now."

The celebrants were impressed and asked how he managed to keep up this rigorous fitness regime.

"You see, my wife and I were married 75 years ago," Old Jonnie explained. "On our wedding night, we made a solemn pledge: Whenever we had a fight, the one who was proved wrong would go outside and take a walk."

Just before the funeral service, the deacon went up to the very elderly widow. He wanted to check some facts for his homily, so he asked her, "Your husband was 98 years old, is that right?"

"That's right," she replied. "He was two years older than me."

"So you're 96?" the deacon asked.

"Yep," the widow responded. "Hardly seems worth my going home after the service, does it, sonny?"

An older nun who was living in a convent next to a construction site noticed the coarse language of the workers and decided to spend some time trying to correct their ways.

She decided she would take her lunch, sit with the workers, and talk with them.

She put a sandwich in a brown bag and walked over to the spot where the men were eating. Sporting a big smile, she walked up to the group and asked: "And do you men know Jesus Christ?" They shook their heads and looked at each other, very confused. One of the workers looked up into the steelworks and yelled out,

"Anybody up there know Jesus Christ?"

One of the workers yelled down, "Yeah, why?"

"His wife's here with his lunch."

At a parish health fair, an elderly gentleman with serious hearing problems learned about a new medical procedure that improved his hearing to almost 100 percent for the first time in many years.

After the surgery, the man's pastor said, "Your family must be really pleased that you can hear again."

The man replies, "Oh, I haven't told my family yet, Father. I just sit around and listen to the family conversations. I've already changed my will three times!"

A very old man lay dying in his bed. In death's doorway, he suddenly smelled the aroma of his favorite chocolate chip cookie wafting up the stairs. The man gathered his remaining strength and lifted himself from the bed. Leaning against the wall, he slowly made his way out of the bedroom, and with even greater effort forced himself down the stairs, gripping the railing with both hands.

With labored breath, he leaned against the doorframe, gazing into the kitchen. Were it not for death's agony, he would have thought himself already in heaven.

There, spread out on the kitchen table, were literally hundreds of his favorite chocolate chip cookies.

Was it heaven? Or was it one final act of heroic love from his devoted wife, seeing to it that he left this world a happy man?

Mustering one great final effort, he threw himself toward the table. The aged and withered hand, shaking, made its way to a cookie at the edge of the table, when he was suddenly smacked with a spatula by his wife.

"Stay out of those," she said. "They're for after the funeral."

———

As they left Mass one Sunday morning, one elderly parishioner remarked, "The choir was awful this morning."

Another said, "The deacon's homily was too long."

The third said, "But you've got to admit, it's not a bad show for only a buck."

A reporter for a local TV station was interviewing an 84-year-old woman who had just gotten married – for the fourth time. The interviewer asked her questions about her new husband. "He's a funeral director," she replied.

The reporter asked if she wouldn't mind talking about her previous husbands and what they did for a living. She paused and then said with a smile that she first married a banker. After he died, she wed a circus ringmaster. Widowed again, she married a man who later became a deacon at her parish. Finally, after she outlived him, she married the funeral director.

The interviewer was quite astonished that she married men with such diverse careers.

"Not at all," she told him. "I married one for the money, two for the show, three to get ready, and four to go!"

Two older men were talking over a cup of coffee at the parish senior center.

"I've sure gotten old," one said. "I've had two bypass surgeries, a hip replacement, new knees, fought prostate cancer and diabetes. I'm half blind, can't hear anything quieter than a jet engine, take 40 different medications that make me dizzy, winded, and subject to blackouts. I have bouts with dementia, poor circulation, hardly feel my hands and feet anymore. I can't even remember if I'm 89 or 98."

"Just thank God you still have your driver's license," said the other.

The Smiths, now in their 80s, were proud of their long family history. Their ancestors had come to America very early. The family lineage had included business and political figures and more than a few priests and bishops. There was even one cardinal.

They decided to compile a family history, a legacy for their children and grandchildren. They hired a fine author. But there was the problem of how to deal the story of Great Uncle George, who had been executed for murder in the electric chair.

The author assured the family he would handle the story as tactfully as possible.

When the book appeared it read, "Great Uncle George occupied a chair of applied electronics at an important government institution and was attached to his position by the strongest of ties. His death came as a great shock."

The parish census taker walked up to a wrinkled little older man rocking in a chair on his porch.

"I couldn't help noticing how happy you look," she said. "What's your secret for a long happy life?"

"I smoke three packs of cigarettes a day," the man boasted. "I also drink a case of whiskey a week, eat fatty foods, and never exercise."

"Wow! That's amazing," said the visitor. "And just how old are you?"

"Twenty-six," the man replied.

A man in Florida, in his 60s, calls his son in Boston one November day.

The father says to the son, "I hate to tell you, but we've got some troubles here in the house. Your mother and I can't stand each other anymore, and we're getting a divorce. I've had it! I want to live out the rest of my years in peace. I'm telling you now, so you and your sister won't go into shock later when I move out."

He hangs up, and the son immediately calls his sister and tells her the news.

The sister says, "I'll handle this."

She phones Florida and says to her father, "Don't do ANYTHING till we get there! We'll all be there Wednesday night."

"All right," the father agrees,

The old man hangs up the phone and hollers to his wife, "OK, they're coming for Thanksgiving. Now, what are we going to tell them to get them to come for Christmas?"

Age had taken its toll on her body, so when the parish's senior center began offering a Stretch-'n-Fit class the elderly woman quickly joined, but just as quickly she was disappointed and quit. When asked what the problem was, she said, "I bent, twisted, gyrated, jumped up and down, and perspired for an hour. But by the time I got my leotard on, the class was over."

A priest was preparing a dying old man for his long journey into the dark night. Whispering firmly, the priest said, "Denounce the devil! Let him know how little you think of his evil."

The dying man said nothing.

The priest repeated his order.

Still the dying man said nothing.

The priest asked, "Why do you refuse to denounce the devil and his evil?"

The dying man said, "Until I know exactly where I'm headin', I don't think I ought to be aggravating NOBODY."

The 95-year-old woman at the nursing home received a visit from the parish's team of Eucharistic ministers.

"How are you feeling?" the visitors asked.

"Oh," said the woman, "I'm just worried sick!"

"What are you worried about, dear?" they asked. "You look like you're in good health. They are taking care of you here, aren't they?"

"Yes, they're taking very good care of me," the woman replied.

"Well, then, what are you worried about?" the visitors asked again.

The woman leaned back in her rocking chair and slowly explained. "Every close friend I ever had has already died and gone on to heaven. I'm afraid they're all wondering where I went."

A wild-eyed man dressed in a Napoleonic costume and hiding his right hand inside his coat entered the office of the Catholic Charities psychiatrist and nervously exclaimed, "I need your help right away."

"I can see that," retorted the counselor. "Sit down and tell me your problem."

"Oh, I don't have a problem," the man snapped. "In fact, as Emperor of France I have everything I could possibly want: money, women, power! But I'm afraid my wife Josephine is in deep mental trouble."

"I see," chuckled the psychiatrist, humoring his obviously deranged patient. "And what seems to be her problem?"

"For some strange reason," answered the man, "she thinks she's married to some guy named Murphy."

The pastor of a remote country parish was having a heart-to-heart talk with an elderly parishioner known for his infrequent appearances at church, whose love of strong drink invariably led to quarrels with his neighbors and occasional shotgun blasts at some of them.

"Can't you see, Ben," asked the priest, "that not one good thing comes out of this drinking?"

"Well, I sort of disagree there," replied the old man. "It makes me miss most of the folks I shoot at."

After decades of devoted service to the ill and dying, three nurses from St. Mary's Hospital went to heaven, and were awaiting their turn with St. Peter to plead their case to enter the Pearly Gates.

The first nurse said, "I worked in the emergency room. We tried our best to help patients. Even though we occasionally did lose one, I think I deserve to go to heaven."

St. Peter looks at her file and admits her.

The second nurse says, "I worked in the operating room. It's a very high stress environment and we do our best. Sometimes patients are too sick and we lose them, but overall we try very hard."

St. Peter looks at her file and admits her.

The third nurse says, "I was a case manager for the hospital's HMO program."

St. Peter looks at her file. He pulls out a calculator and starts punching away furiously, constantly going back to the nurse's file. After a few minutes St. Peter looks up, smiles, and says, "Congratulations! You've been admitted to heaven…but you can only stay for five days."

During the parish celebration for his 104th birthday, Old Jonnie was asked: "What is the best thing about being 104?"

Jonnie smiled and replied, "No peer pressure."

Old Jonnie walked into a Catholic book and gift shop. Near the cash register he saw a display of baseball caps with "WWJD" printed on all of them. He was puzzled over what the letters could mean, so he asked the clerk.

The clerk explained that the letters stood for "What Would Jesus Do" and were meant to inspire people to imagine how Jesus would act in a similar situation.

Old Jonnie thought a moment and then replied, "Well, I don't think Jesus would pay $24.95 for one of these silly hats."

The retired pastor called his doctor. "Is it true," he asked, "that the medication you prescribed for me has to be taken for the rest of my life?

"Yes, Monsignor," the doctor assured the priest, "I'm afraid so."

After a few moments of silence, the priest said, "Well, Doc, I guess I should be ready to go after serving God all my life."

"What are you talking about?" asked the doctor.

The priest said, "My prescription is marked *No refills!*"

**Age seldom arrives smoothly or quickly.
It is more often a succession of jerks.**

Who said seniors can't keep up with the times? The staff at St. Monica's Senior Center gives residents a course in new technology, like phone texting, so grandparents can understand their grandchildren as well as communicate with other seniors. Here are a few of their hints:

ATD: At The Doctor's

BFF: Best Friend Fell

BTW: Bring The Wheelchair

BYOT: Bring Your Own Teeth

CBM: Covered By Medicare

DWI: Driving While Incontinent

FWIW: Forgot Where I Was

FYI: Found Your Insulin

GGLKI: Gotta Go, Laxative Kicking In

GGPBL: Gotta Go, Pacemaker Battery Low

GHA: Got Heartburn Again

IMHO?: Is My Hearing Aid On?

LMDO: Laughing My Dentures Out

LOL: Living On Lipitor

ROFL...CGU: Rolling On Floor Laughing...Can't Get Up

TTYL: Talk To You Louder

WAITT?: Who Am I Talking To?

WTP?: Where's The Prunes?

WWNO: Walker Wheels Need Oil

The parish hired an aggressive fund-raising consultant to handle the drive for the new church building. The young woman was great at persuading parishioners to contribute. But she was stymied by one penny-pinching senior citizen named "Old Jonnie."

One day, the fundraiser finally cornered Old Jonnie and asked him why he wouldn't donate to the new church building.

"It's true that we senior citizens are much more valuable than younger generations," Old Jonnie told her. "But it's not in money."

"What is it then?" she demanded.

"We have silver in our hair, gold in our teeth, stones in our kidneys, and lead in our feet. And we're just loaded with natural gas!"

———

Old Jonnie was talking to his pastor. He said. "When you get to my age you spend a lot more time thinking about the hereafter."

"It's pretty normal to think about life after death," said the pastor.

"Well, that's not exactly what I meant," replied Old Jonnie. "I often find myself going into a room and wondering what I came in here after."

———

**One must wait until evening
to see how splendid the day has been.**

PART TWO

JOKES ABOUT RELATIONSHIPS

Marriage is a sacrament that comes with the graces of a loving God. But relationship – ahh, that's a little different. Relationship is best handled with a sense of humor. Laughter – and its companion, irony – is the best medicine to carry us through the inevitable rough spots.

The eternal conflict – sometimes gentle, sometimes raucous – that exists between couples can be a source of pain, certainly. But just as certainly it can be the source of great humor. As long as we don't take ourselves too seriously, of course.

The jokes and stories that follow poke fun at the division – or lack thereof – of household duties, at miscommunication, at the tussles and stumblings that punctuate married life. Nor should we ever neglect the omnipresent mother-in-law jokes. After all, without marriage there would be no such thing as in-laws, and then where would we humorists be?

Like a cartoonist's caricature, relationship jokes can highlight a flaw, draw humor from a miscue, or find a smile in a conflict. While human relationships are truly a divine gift, it is also a great gift to be able to discover a smile or laugh in them. Humor celebrates the real bond of commitment that allows couples to stay together.

Enjoy these slices of relationship humor, many with a specifically Catholic twist.

**Keep your eyes wide open before the wedding,
and half shut afterwards.**

A man and his wife are having an argument about who should brew the coffee each morning.

Wife says, "You should do it, because you get up first, and then we don't have to wait as long to get our coffee."

Husband says, "You are in charge of cooking around here and you should do it, because that is your job, and I can just wait for my coffee."

Wife replies, "No, you should do it, and besides, it is in the Bible that the man should make the coffee."

Husband answers, "I can't believe that; show me."

So she fetched the Bible, and opened the New Testament and showed him that at the top of several pages it indeed says:

"HEBREWS."

———

One year a husband decided to buy his mother-in-law a plot at the Gate of Heaven Cemetery as a Christmas gift. The next year, he didn't buy her anything.

When his wife asked him why, he replied, "Well, she still hasn't used the gift I bought her last year!"

———

Never go to bed mad. Stay up and fight.

It was my wife's 25th reunion of her graduating class at St. Patrick's High School. We were sitting at a table and she kept staring at a drunken man swigging his drink as he sat alone at a nearby table.

I asked her, "Do you know him?"

"Yes," she sighed. "He's my old boyfriend. I understand he took to drinking right after we split up those many years ago, and I hear he hasn't been sober since."

"My God," I said, "who'd think anyone could go on celebrating that long?"

———

The hospital chaplain sits outside the emergency room with a husband whose wife has just been admitted. The chaplain says in a very concerned voice, "I don't like the looks of your wife at all."

"Me neither, Father," said the husband. "But she's a great cook and really good with the kids."

———

While shopping for vacation clothes, the president of the parish council and his wife passed a display of bathing suits. She asked him, "What do you think? Should I get a bikini or an all-in-one?"

"Better get a bikini," he replied. "You'd never get it all in one."

He's still in intensive care.

At a reception for new members of the parish, the deacon asked one of the women, "Aren't you wearing your wedding ring on the wrong finger?"

The woman replied, "Yes, I am. I married the wrong man."

On the way home from Mass one Sunday, a married couple quarreled badly. The wife said to her husband, "You know, I was a fool when I married you."

The husband replied, "Yes, dear, but I was in love and didn't notice."

Father Joel, who was a bit absent-minded, thought he was prepared for the wedding. When he went to call the couple up to the altar, however, he couldn't remember their names. So he tried to disguise his memory loss and said, "Will those wanting to get married please come forward?"

Nine single women, three widows, four widowers, and six single men stepped to the front.

A good wife always forgives her husband when she's wrong.

At the reception in the church hall following the nuptial Mass, the father of the bride made an announcement: "I would like to thank you all for coming here today to celebrate my daughter's wedding. The seating arrangement for the reception has been specially organized so that all of the people that bought large presents are seated in front and those who bought smaller gifts are at the back."

Uncle Fred raised his hand. "What if you forgot to bring anything?"

"You're serving the food," said the father.

Although married for many years, Paul had been ignored lately by his wife, Liz. During a counseling session with their parish priest, Paul said, "Come on, Liz, admit it. You only married me because my granddad left me six million dollars, didn't you?"

"You really are silly, Paul," retorted Liz. "I couldn't care less who left it to you."

Quietly watching the exchange, the priest leaned over to both of them and asked for a donation to the building fund.

**Marriage is a very expensive way
to get your laundry done for free.**

At a parish celebration for couples reaching their 50th year of married life together, Nick was asked to give a brief account of the benefits of being married so long.

"Tell us, Nick, just what is it you have learned from all those wonderful years with your wife?"

Nick responded, "Well, I've learned that marriage is the greatest teacher of all. It teaches you forbearance, meekness, self-restraint, loyalty, forgiveness, and a great many other qualities you wouldn't have needed if you'd have stayed single."

———

Deacon John wanted to get his wife, Carole, something nice for their wedding anniversary. He settled on one of the newest smart cell phones. Carole, not very technologically adept, was excited and loved the phone, especially after John explained all the features.

The following day after Mass, Carole went shopping. Her phone rang, and it was her husband, John.

"Hi, Carole," he said. "How do you like your new phone?"

Carole replies, "I just love it, John. It's so small and light and your voice is clear as a bell, but there's one feature I really don't understand."

"What's that?" asked John.

"How did the phone know I'd be at the Wal-Mart?"

"Hello, Bill," said Jim, meeting a buddy for the first time in a long while. "Did you marry that girl you used to go with or are you still doing your own cooking and ironing?"

"Yes," replied Bill.

———

As they were making final arrangements for the wedding Mass on Saturday, the groom-to-be's uncle said to him: "Congratulations, my boy! I'm sure you'll look back and remember today as the happiest day of your life."

"But I'm not getting married until tomorrow," his nephew protested.

"I know," replied the uncle.

———

During the reception following the wedding Mass, the disc jockey polled the guests to see who had been married longest. There was a couple who had been married 55 years. The DJ asked, "What advice would you give to the newly married couple?"

The woman said, "The three most important words in a marriage are, 'You're probably right.'"

Everyone looked at the husband, who said immediately, "She's probably right."

During a Reconciliation service before an upcoming wedding, the mother of the bride confessed to the priest that she just learned that the groom's mother had bought the exact same dress she had for the wedding.

"I'm so mad I could just kill her; that dress cost me a fortune," the woman told the priest. But then she said, "Don't worry, Father. I don't really mean that. I'll just go and buy another dress to wear to the ceremony."

"But what will you do with that expensive dress?" the priest asked. "Won't you ever use it?"

"Who said I won't use it?" said the woman. "I'll just wear it to the rehearsal dinner."

A young bride-and-groom-to-be had just selected the wedding ring. As the girl admired her band of gold, the boy suddenly looked concerned.

"Tell me," he asked the elderly salesman, "is there anything special I'll have to do to take care of this ring?"

With a fatherly smile, the salesman said, "One of the best ways to protect your wedding ring, son, is to dip it in dishwater three times a day."

A husband stepped on one of those scales that tell your fortune and weight and dropped in a coin. "Look at this," he said to his wife, showing her a small, white card. "It says I'm energetic, bright, resourceful, and a great lover."

"Yeah," his wife nodded, "and it's got your weight wrong, too."

A couple was traveling overseas when their parish priest e-mailed some sad news: "Peg's mother passed away in her sleep. Did you wish to have her embalmed and buried or cremated?"

Back came the man's reply, "Take no chances. Order all three."

A man and woman are having problems a very short time after the wedding and decide to seek an annulment. The deacon handling the paperwork asks the husband, "What has brought you both to the point where you are not able to keep this marriage together?"

The husband replies, "In the six weeks we've been together, we haven't been able to agree on a single thing."

The wife says, "Seven weeks."

As they celebrated the 25ᵗʰ renewal of their wedding vows at church in front of all their friends and family, the man asked his wife what she'd like for her anniversary.

"I'd love to be six again," she replied.

The next morning, he got her up bright and early and off they went to a local theme park. What a day! He put her on every ride in the park: the Death Slide, the Screaming Loop, the Wall of Fear.

Five hours later she staggered out of the theme park, her head reeling and her stomach upside down. Right to McDonald's they went, where her husband ordered her a Big Mac along with extra fries and a refreshing chocolate shake.

Then it was off to a movie, the latest Star Wars epic, and hot dogs, popcorn, cola, and candy. Finally she wobbled home with her husband and collapsed into bed.

He leaned over and lovingly asked, "Well, dear, what was it like being six again?"

One eye opened. The wife said, "I meant my dress size!"

**Men who have a pierced ear
are better prepared for marriage.
They've already bought jewelry
and experienced pain.**

On their way home from an unsuccessful counseling session with their parish priest, a couple drove several miles down a country road, not saying a word. The earlier discussion had led to an argument, and neither wanted to concede their position.

As they passed a barnyard of mules and pigs, the husband sarcastically asked, "Relatives of yours?"

"Yep," the wife replied. "In-laws."

More quotes for discussion from a parish marriage enrichment program:

- "I just got back from a pleasure trip. I took my mother-in-law to the airport."

- "Someone stole all my credit cards, but I won't be reporting it. The thief spends less than my spouse does."

- "She was at the beauty shop for two hours before Easter. That was only for the estimate."

- "He says he finds God on the golf course instead of at Mass, but that's only because he keeps taking his name in vain out there."

The priest considered himself a pretty good golfer. One Wednesday afternoon he was at his favorite course ready to tee off when another golfer approached and asked if he could join him. The priest said he usually played alone, but agreed to the twosome. The two men were even after the first couple holes and the second guy said, "We're about evenly matched, Father. How about playing for five bucks a hole?" The priest admitted he wasn't much for betting, but agreed to the wager, but the second guy won the remaining sixteen holes with ease.

As they were walking off the 18th green, the winner counted his $80 in winnings. Suddenly he thought better of it and tried to hand the money back to the priest.

The priest said, "You won fair and square, and I was foolish to bet with you. You keep your winnings."

The other guy said, "That's very nice of you, Father. Is there anything I can do to make it up to you?"

The priest said, "Well, you could come to Mass on Sunday and make a donation. And, if you want to bring your mother and father along, I'll marry them."

———

Adam and Eve were the happiest couple in the world. Neither had a mother-in-law.

A boy comes home from Catholic school and tells his mother he has a part in the class play.

She asks, "What part is it?"

The boy says, "I get to play the part of a husband."

The mother scowls and says, "Go back and tell the teacher you want a speaking part."

While creating husbands, God promised women that good and ideal husbands would be found in all corners of the world.

And then he made the earth round.

As the man was driving down the freeway trying to get to a senior citizen meeting at church, his car phone rang. Answering, he heard his wife's voice urgently warning him, "I just heard on the news that there's a car going the wrong way on I-280. Please be careful!"

"It's not just one car!" screamed the man. "It's hundreds of them!"

**I was married by a judge;
I should have asked for a jury.**

A couple was celebrating 50 years together. Their three kids, all very successful financially, agreed to a Sunday dinner in their honor after Mass.

"Happy anniversary, Mom and Dad," gushed son number one. "Sorry I'm running late. I had an emergency at the hospital with a patient, and I didn't have time to get you a gift."

"Not to worry," said the mother. "The important thing is that we're all together today."

Son number two arrived and announced, "You and Mom look great, Dad. I just flew in from Los Angeles between depositions and didn't have time to shop for you."

"It's nothing," said the father. "We're glad you were able to come."

Just then the daughter arrived. "Hello and happy anniversary, Mom and Dad! I'm sorry, but my boss is sending me out of town and I was really busy packing so I didn't have time to get you anything."

"Hey, we understand," said the mother. "We're both just so proud of you."

After they'd finished dessert, however, the father said, "There's something your mother and I have wanted to tell you for a long time. You see, when we got together we were very poor, and throughout the years your mother and I knew that we loved each other very much, but we just never found the time to get married."

The three children gasped and all three started to say at once, "You mean we're...?"

But the father interrupted them and said, "Yep, and cheap ones, too."

Susie's husband had been slipping in and out of a coma for several months, prompting frequent visits by their parish priest. Things looked grim, but she was by his bedside every single day. One day as he slipped back into consciousness, he motioned for her to come near. She pulled the chair close to the bed and leaned her ear close to be able to hear him.

"You know" he whispered, his eyes filling with tears, "you have been with me through all the bad times. When I got fired, you stuck right beside me. When my business went under, there you were. When we lost the house, you were there. My health started failing, you were still by my side. And you know what?"

"What, dear?" she asked gently.

"I've decided you're bad luck."

It's all in the punctuation: An English professor at Notre Dame University wrote the words, "Woman without her man is nothing," on the blackboard and directed his students to punctuate it correctly.

The men wrote: "Woman, without her man, is nothing."

The women wrote: "Woman: Without her, man is nothing."

Old Jonnie was known among his friends to be very brief and to the point. He really never said too much.

One day, a woman selling cosmetics knocked on his door and asked to see his wife. Jonnie told her that his wife wasn't home.

"Well," replied the insistent saleswoman, "could I please wait for her?"

Jonnie directed her to the front room and left her there for more than three hours.

The saleswoman was getting really angry, so she called to Jonnie in the other room and asked, "May I know where your wife is?"

"She went to Queen of Peace Cemetery," he replied.

"And when is she returning?"

"I don't really know," he said. "She's been there 11 years now."

———

A man and a friend are playing golf one day at their local golf course. One of the guys is about to chip onto the green when he sees a long funeral procession on the road next to the course heading for Queen of Heaven Cemetery. He stops in mid-swing, takes off his golf cap, closes his eyes, and bows down in prayer.

His friend says, "Wow, that is the most thoughtful and touching thing I have ever seen. You truly are a kind and thoughtful man."

The man then replies, "Yeah, well, we were married 35 years."

Three young boys were walking on the sidewalk arguing over whose daddy was the greatest. One said, "My dad is the greatest because he is the president of the town bank." The second boy said, "That is pretty good, but my daddy owns two grocery stores in town!" The third boy said, "That's nothing, my dad is a deacon, and he owns hell. He came home last night and told my mom that the parish council gave it to him!"

A husband asked to talk to the parish priest about his marriage. He said, "When we were first married, I would come home from the office and my wife would bring my slippers and our cute little dog would run around barking. Now, after ten years, it's all different. I come home, the dog brings the slippers, and my wife runs around barking."

"What's the problem?" said the priest. "You're still getting the same service."

**I love being married:
It's so great to finally find
that one special person
you want to annoy for the rest of your life.**

A woman accompanied her husband to the doctor's office. After his checkup, the doctor asked the wife to step into his office alone. He said, "Your husband is suffering from a very severe stress disorder. If you don't do the following, your husband will surely die. Each morning I want you to fix him a healthy breakfast. Be pleasant at all times. For lunch make him a nutritious meal. For dinner prepare an especially nice meal for him. Pray for him constantly. Don't burden him with chores. Don't discuss your problems with him; it will only make his stress worse. No nagging. If you can do this for the next ten months to a year, I think your husband will regain his health completely."

On the way home, the husband asked his wife. "What did the doctor say?"

"He said you're going to die," she replied.

———

At the parish charismatic prayer meeting a woman stood up and witnessed: "We are all living in a wicked land where sin is on every hand. I have had a terrible fight with the devil every day this week."

Her husband, who was sitting glumly by her side, said, "She's not that easy to get along with either."

"Honey," said this husband to his wife, "I invited a new friend home for supper."

"What? Are you crazy?" said his wife. "The house is a mess, I haven't been shopping, all the dishes are dirty, and I don't feel like cooking a fancy meal!"

"I know all that," said the husband, "but it is our newly ordained associate at the parish and he's going to be doing marriage counseling. I wanted him to see what married life is really like."

My Dearest Susan,

Sweetie of my heart. I've been so desolate ever since I broke off our engagement. Simply devastated. Won't you please consider coming back to me? You hold a place in my heart no other woman can fill. I can never find another woman quite like you. I need you so much. Won't you forgive me and let us make a new beginning? I love you so.

Yours always and truly,

John

P.S. Congratulations on you winning the lottery.

**I married Mr. Right.
I just didn't know his first name was Always.**

A woman found herself standing at the Pearly Gates. St. Peter greeted her and said, "These are the Gates to Heaven, my dear. But you must do one more thing before you can enter."

The woman was very excited, and asked St. Peter what she must do.

"Spell a word," St. Peter replied.

"What word?" she asked.

"Any word," answered St. Peter. "It's your choice."

The woman promptly replied, "Then the word I will spell is love: L-O-V-E."

St. Peter welcomed her in, and asked her if she would mind taking his place at the gates for a few minutes while he took a break. So the woman was sitting in St. Peter's chair when a man approached the gates. She realized it was her husband of many years.

"What happened?" she cried. "Why are you here?"

Her husband stared at her for a moment, then said, "I was so upset when I left your funeral that I got in an accident. Did I really make it to heaven?"

"Not yet," she replied. "You must spell a word first."

"What word?" he asked.

The woman responded, "Czechoslovakia."

A mild-mannered man was tired of being bossed around by his wife so he went to a counselor at Catholic Charities for help.

The counselor said he needed to build his self-esteem, and gave him a book on assertiveness, which he read on the way home.

By the time he got home he had finished the book.

The man stormed into the house and walked up to his wife.

Pointing a finger in her face, he said, "From now on, I want you to know that I am the man of this house, and my word is law! I want you to prepare me a gourmet meal tonight, and when I'm finished eating my meal, I expect a sumptuous dessert. Then, after dinner, you're going to draw me my bath so I can relax. And when I'm finished with my bath, guess who's going to dress me and comb my hair?"

"The funeral director," said his wife.

A man was just waking up from anesthesia after surgery at St. Vincent Hospital, and his wife was sitting by his side. His eyes fluttered open and he said, "You're beautiful." Then he fell asleep again. His wife, who had never heard him say that before, stayed by his side.

A few minutes later his eyes fluttered open and he said, "You're cute."

The wife was disappointed and asked, "What happened to beautiful?"

The man replied, "The drugs are wearing off."

It was an Italian family tradition that when someone died, the relatives passed by the open casket at the funeral home and threw in money. The old man had developed into quite a miser and told his wife that he wanted the tradition fulfilled when he passed away. And so she promised him, with all her heart, that when he died she would obey.

Not long afterward, the man did, in fact, die. He was laid out in an open casket and sure enough people put in many dollars bills and even some fives and tens. When the wake was over and just before the funeral director closed the casket, the widow said, "Wait. I want to be alone with him for a moment." She went over to bid her husband a final farewell.

At the cemetery after the funeral, her best friend came up to her and offered a word of comfort. Then she said, "I hope you were not fool enough to leave all that money in there with your husband."

The loyal wife replied, "Listen, I couldn't go back on my word. I promised him that I was going to let people put that money in the casket with him and that's what I did."

"What a waste of money," said the friend.

"Oh, I don't know," said the widow. "I took out the cash and wrote him a check."

———

Catholic wisdom: Laugh and the whole world laughs with you; snore and you'll wake up the person in the next pew.

A young husband with an inferiority complex insisted he was just a little pebble on a vast beach.

The marriage counselor, trying to be creative, told him, "If you wish to save your marriage, you'd better be a little boulder."

———

Jack is a busy, hard-working guy. In addition to his demanding job at the bank, he's a deacon at the local parish. But he loves his wife and always wants to do the right thing by her.

Jill says to him, "Jack, that young couple that just moved in next door seem like such a loving twosome. Every morning, when he leaves the house, he kisses her goodbye; and every evening when he comes home he brings her a dozen roses. Now, why can't you do that?"

"Gosh," Jack says, "I hardly know the girl."

———

Q: Is it all right to bring a date to the wedding?

A: Not if you are the bride or groom.

———

**The most effective way
to remember your wife's birthday
is to forget it once.**

It was only a few weeks after their lavish wedding at St. Mary's when the newlywed wife said to her husband, "I have great news. Pretty soon, there's going to be three in this house instead of two."

Her husband held her with a smile on his face and delight in his eyes.

"That is wonderful news, honey," he said.

"I'm so glad you feel that way about Mom moving in, dear."

———

A deacon was as passionate about golf as he was about his faith. One day he and his wife walked into the office of his dentist, a parishioner. The deacon said to the dentist, "Doc, I'm in one heck of a hurry. I have two buddies out in my car waiting for us to go play golf, so forget about the anesthetic. I don't have time to wait for the gums to get numb. I just want you to pull the tooth and be done with it! We have a 10 a.m. tee time at the best golf course in town and it's 9:30 already."

The dentist thought, "My goodness, what a brave guy, asking to have his tooth pulled with nothing to kill the pain." So he asked, "Which tooth is it, deacon?"

The man turned to his wife and said, "Open your mouth, honey, and show him."

A police officer in a small town stopped a motorist who was speeding down Main Street toward the local Catholic Church.

"But, officer," the young man began, "I can explain…."

"Just be quiet," snapped the officer. "I'm going to let you cool your heels in jail until the chief gets back."

"But, officer, I just wanted to say…."

"And I said to keep quiet! You're going to jail!"

A few hours later the officer looked in on his prisoner and said, "Lucky for you the chief's at his daughter's wedding. He'll be in a good mood when he gets back."

"Don't count on it," answered the fellow in the cell glumly. "I'm the groom."

———

There was once a wife so jealous that when her husband came home one night and she couldn't find hairs on his jackets she yelled at him, "Great, so now you're cheating on me with a bald woman!"

———

**Just think, if it weren't for marriage,
men would go through life
thinking they had no faults at all.**

Translations from "Woman-talk" to "Man-talk" (and vice versa):

When the woman says: You want.
She means: You want.

When she says: We need.
She means: I want.

When she says: It's your decision.
She means: The correct decision should be obvious.

When she says: Do what you want.
She means: You'll pay for this later.

When she says: We need to talk.
She means: I need to talk.

When she says: Sure…go ahead.
She means: Over my dead body.

When she says: I'm not upset.
She means: I'm upset.

When she says: This kitchen is so inconvenient.
She means: I want a new house.

When she says: Hang the picture there.
She means: Don't hang the picture there.

When she says: Am I fat?
She means: Tell me I'm beautiful.

When she says: You have to communicate.
She means: You have to agree with me.

When she says: Nothing is wrong.
She means: Everything is wrong.

When she says: Nothing is wrong, really.
She means: You're an idiot if you don't know what's wrong.

When the man says, "Huh?"
He means: "Huh?"

Some people asked Old Jonnie the secret of his long marriage: "We always took time to go to a restaurant two weeknights every week. We'd have a nice candlelight dinner, listen to soft music, and take a slow walk home. She went on Tuesdays and Fridays, I went on Mondays and Thursdays."

**To be happy with a man,
you must understand him a lot
and love him a little.**

**To be happy with a woman,
you must love her a lot
and not try to understand her at all.**

The Catholic marriage counselor asked her client, "Now, sir, what seems to be troubling you?"

The man replied: "Well, it all started when I married a widow with a grown daughter who then became my stepdaughter. My dad came to visit us, fell in love with my lovely stepdaughter, then married her. And so my stepdaughter was now my stepmother. Soon, my wife had a son who was, of course, my daddy's brother-in-law since he is the half-brother of my stepdaughter, who is now, of course, my daddy's wife. Now, since my new son is brother to my stepmother, he also became my uncle. As you know, my wife is my step-grandmother since she is my stepmother's mother. And don't forget that my stepmother is my stepdaughter. Remember, too, that I am my wife's grandson."

"Well," said the counselor, but the man cut her off.

"But hold on just a few minutes more," he said. "You see, since I'm married to my step-grandmother, I am not only the wife's grandson and her hubby, but I am also my own grandfather. Now can you understand why I'm talking to a Catholic counselor?"

"Not really," said the counselor.

"Well, I want to see if I'm eligible to get an annulment."

————

**Marriage is a relationship
in which one person is usually right
and the other is usually the husband.**

A couple met with a Catholic counselor to resolve communication problems in their marriage. The fighting and bickering during the session got so bad the counselor called for a timeout and told them he was ending the session early but had an assignment for each of them.

The counselor told the husband: "You're an athletic guy. I want you to jog 10 miles every day for the next 30 days. Work off some of that frustration."

To the wife he said: "You are just too uptight. I want you to stay home and eat some comfort food and watch nothing but sitcoms on TV."

Then he told them to call him at the end of the 30 days and let him know how things were going.

Thirty days later, the husband called the counselor very excited. "I did just as you said and I have never felt better in my life," he exclaimed over the phone.

"Great!" replied the counselor. "And how's your wife?"

The man paused and then said, "How should I know? I'm 300 miles from home!"

Father: Don't you think our son gets his brains from me?

Mother: Probably, dear. I still have all of mine.

Ted and Alice were married at St. Mary's Church and immediately left on their honeymoon.

When they got back, Alice's mother asked, "How was it?"

"Oh, Ma," Alice replied, "the honeymoon was wonderful. So romantic." But then she burst into tears.

"But as soon as we returned home," she cried, "Ted started using the most ghastly language, saying things I've never heard before! I mean, all these awful four-letter words!"

"Calm down, Alice," said her mother. "Tell me which four-letter words he said."

Still sobbing, Alice whispered, "Oh, Ma...words like dust, wash, cook, and iron. He even said I should go to *work!*"

———

Molly and Peter have been married for almost 48 years and have raised a brood of 12 children and are blessed with 23 grandchildren.

When asked the secret for staying together all that time, Molly replies, "Many years ago we made a promise to each other: The first to pack up and leave has to take all the kids."

———

**I haven't spoken to my wife in eighteen months;
I don't like to interrupt her.**

I just bumped into my old friend Mike. We chatted and he surprised me by saying that he and his wife, Emily, were talking to a marriage counselor at Catholic Charities.

"What happened?" I asked. "You two seemed so happy together."

"Well," Mike said, "ever since we got married, Emily has tried to change me. She got me to stop drinking, smoking, and running around. She taught me how to dress well, enjoy the fine arts, cook gourmet food, listen to classical music, and invest in the stock market."

"And you're bitter because she did all that," I asked.

"No, of course not," said Mike. "It's just that now I feel Emily isn't good enough for me."

A newlywed husband and wife were at a party chatting with some friends when the subject of marriage counseling came up.

"Oh, we'll never need that," the young woman said. "My husband and I have a great relationship. He was a communications major in college and I majored in theatre arts. He communicates really well, and I act like I'm listening."

A marriage is like a fire.
It tends to go out if unattended.

ABOUT THE AUTHORS
Deacon Tom Sheridan

As a veteran secular newspaperman, Tom Sheridan developed a keen eye for the humor in life. A deacon ordained in 1979 for the Diocese of Joliet, Illinois, and a former editor of the Archdiocese of Chicago's newspaper and other publications, Deacon Tom also knows a little about the humor to be found in religion. And as a husband and father of five children and several grandchildren, he believes humor will help see us all through our various struggles. He writes from Ocala, Florida, where he lives with his wife, Kathy. He is the author of three other books in the Catholic Jokes series, *The Gift of Baptism*, and *The Gift of Godparents* for ACTA Publications.

Father James Martin, SJ

James Martin, SJ, is a Jesuit priest, culture editor of *America* magazine, and author of several books, including *Jesus: A Pilgrimage* and *My Life with the Saints*, which was named a "Best Book" of the year by *Publishers Weekly*, and *The New York Times* bestseller *The Jesuit Guide to (Almost) Everything*. He is the author of *Between Heaven and Mirth: Why Joy, Humor and Laughter Are at the Heart of the Spiritual Life*. Father Martin is a frequent commentator on religion and spirituality in the media. Among other periodicals he has written for *The New York Times* and *The Wall Street Journal*, and he blogs for HuffingtonPost.com. He has appeared on all the major television and radio networks; on CNN, the BBC, Vatican Radio, and the History Channel; as well as in venues as diverse as National Public Radio's "Fresh Air with Terry Gross," Fox TV's "The O'Reilly Factor," and Comedy Central's "The Colbert Report."

Also Available from ACTA Publications

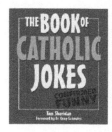
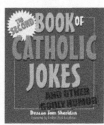